Aging Matters

Visit www.booksurge.com to order additional copies.

DANIEL J. MONAHAN, LMSW

AGING MATTERS

LOVES, LAUGHS & LOSSES

2007

Aging Matters

Dedicated to DADACBNT

Hey, Ommy, I Know You're There

TABLE OF CONTENTS

ACKNOWLEDGEMENTS

There are individuals without whom this book would not look as it does. Good eyes, good ears and good hearts make for good friends. From word choice to punctuation and spelling, their thoughtful, insightful suggestions energize the pages. I owe a debt of gratitude to the following: my wife, Annie; my oldest, Dan Jr.; as well as, Ron Becker, Lois Schram, Robert Shauer, Pat Tomasso and John White. You have my thanks.

The four nursing homes which granted me interviewing access to their staff represent their industry well. After all, the stories you are about to read are brought to life every day in long-term care facilities from New York to California. Many thanks, much love and great respect to all who have chosen to perform the important and challenging work of caring for our elderly in nursing homes, especially those from:

Beth Abraham Health Services
Crown Nursing and Rehabilitation Center
Greater Harlem Nursing Home
Schervier Nursing Care Center

And then there's one, my youngest. Tim is the man. He was there at every turn and I am grateful for the time we shared. Thanks T-Rock.

AUTHOR'S NOTE

Although no release of Protected Health Information occurs, two additional steps have been implemented to ensure confidentiality and privacy for each of the residents discussed and written about; the name of the facility in which any one interview was conducted is not identified, and fictitious names are used for all residents.

The anecdotes attributed to participating staff members, while not necessarily indicative of the actual sequence of conversation during the interviews, certainly represent the essence of their contributions.

FOREWORD

Dan's work is a beautiful reminder for all of us once connected, now connected, or who at some time will be connected to a nursing home. *Aging Matters: Loves, Laughs & Losses* makes it clear that what we, as educators, have the joy of touching, is the core of our students, that energy which keeps them committed and dedicated to caring for their residents. Thank you Dan, for sharing the words and hearts of those who are often minimized by their titles, and for putting the focus where it should be, on the devoted staff in our nursing homes.

Lois Schram
L/S Gerontology Seminars
Schramski@aol.com

INTRODUCTION

Welcome home. Just hear these two words and you immediately feel safe and warm. Trust and confidence flourish. Relationships, grounded in unconditional love, support and challenge you. Familiarity abounds and comforts. It's in the faces, voices and touches found in your daily routines. Truly, it is good to be admitted.

That's right, admitted. Home for nearly one and a half million Americans is a nursing home. The source of their safety and warmth, unconditional love and familiarity, as always at home, is family. Here, however, family is comprised of caregivers: Nursing Assistants, Nurses, Doctors, Social Workers, Recreation Leaders, Dieticians, Housekeepers, Maintenance Workers and Physical, Occupational and Speech Therapists. Together, they provide over thirteen billion hours of care in this country each year. And they do so as *family*.

There is a story for each reader among these more than two hundred accounts of relationships rich in love and devotion. Each of you can glean your own connection as you share in the experiences of those who care for our elderly and infirm. For residents, their loved ones and caregivers, past and present, they are sure to stir fond memories. Future residents and those close to them can be comforted with the knowledge that such kindred souls await their arrival.

An emotional journey, the interview process laid bare intimate everyday exchanges and connections between nursing home residents and their caregivers. Staff members reflections' conjured memories of profound joy and sadness and communicated a deep personal and professional commitment to those they serve. Their stories are heartwarming and inspiring, each revealing a willingness to be vulnerable and, in that vulnerability, a capacity to love seemingly without bounds.

It is time for me to say thank you and allow their words to touch your hearts as they have touched mine. There is much peace of mind within their stories. While my words here thank all who contributed to this book, my hope is the book thanks all who contribute daily to the well-being of our nursing home residents across this great land. I consider it a privilege to have been granted such access and a pleasure to welcome you. For all of us, aging matters.

Dear Staff Members,

My request was simple enough. Describe your work through a story that depicts a resident relationship. Your responses were gentle, powerful, poignant, sometimes painful or even hysterical, and anything but simple. Never before has the phrase *"it's the journey, not the destination"* so resonated. My lesson is that life itself is the gift, to be cherished and nurtured, unconditionally. There is no age, ethnicity, religion, disability, financial status, behavior, nothing whatsoever, which precludes one from your love. What a journey, indeed.

Along the way we connected. This seems a habit of yours. The ease with which you love is quite moving. I felt your warmth and vulnerability when speaking of current residents and your pain and sadness when you spoke of residents past. Welcomed and made comfortable, we laughed hard and cried harder.

Though I penned these stories, you authored the story. While my writing is complete, your work goes on. Daily, the extended family grows as you continue in dedicated service. On behalf of those you provide care and their families, thank you. I will miss each of you (I already do).

Love,
Dan

Dear Family Member,

How frightened you were the day your loved one was admitted. We remember your nervous energy, your rapid-fire questions and your tears. Though there was some comfort in our words, we knew most would come only with time. Leaving for home that first night was nearly impossible, your feelings of abandoning almost unbearable. Your trust, now well earned, was in strangers that day, a depth of vulnerability hard to imagine.

To serve is an honor and a privilege. The relationships which develop, the closeness we feel with those we provide care, are remarkable to see when individuals from such diverse cultures come together as one family, one of which you are a member. The work is hard and, equally so, important. We are grateful for the opportunity to love your loved one. It is truly a blessing.

Our losses are humbling. Together, we miss many who taught us much—about themselves, about you, and about ourselves. We hope to share what has been given to us— lifetimes of memories filled with *Loves, Laughs and Losses*—and to say thank you.

Love,
The Staff

LOVES

Love is patient, love is kind.

It is not jealous, it is not pompous, it is not inflated, it is not rude.

It does not seek its own interests, it is not quick-tempered, it does not brood over injury.

It does not rejoice over wrongdoing but rejoices with the truth.

It bears all things, believes all things, hopes all things, endures all things.

Love never fails.

1 Corinthians 13:4-8

from Marie, CNA...

It is my heart to take care of them. I learn a lot from them. I'm so proud to work with them.

* * *

from Emeka, Nurse...

For five years I arrived to work at 3p.m. to the same daily greeting. "What's up dude?," Lorna would ask. To which I'd respond, "What are we going to do today?" And Lorna would answer invariably, "Same old, I'll be back," and away she would walk.

Later in the evening I would say to her as she wandered by, "You said you were coming back." Lorna would stay stoically, "There's a lot going on here," meaning she's busy. My standard reply was to say, "I see you mopping the floor," referring to her never-ending wandering. Lorna would laugh out loud.

She was always last in and first out of the dining room. One night Lorna finished dinner, ate everything as always, but remained in the dining room. When I approached her she said she didn't feel well. We took her to her room where we lost her. It was only one month ago and it is still very, very difficult. I find myself looking for her as I arrive. I miss her very much.

* * *

from Mustafa, Nurse...

I have taken care of Daisy for one year. Although she is

non-verbal, when I talk to her, her eyes talk to me. She has bright eyes that smile and cry. Daisy has touched me.

* * *

from Barbara, Therapeutic Recreation Leader...

Daphne was my sixth grade teacher. We remained close throughout my high school years. When I was in her class I got a D in conduct on my report card. We were talking about it after school and I told her I knew I'd earned it, but that if I wasn't in school the next day, she'd know what happened. Daphne changed the D to a B.

When she was admitted to the nursing home I recognized her immediately. She was so excited to have a former student taking care of her. This was someone who had given to me all my life. Now I would give to her.

Yet, she taught me one more lesson before leaving this world. As she was actively dying, I would spend my break time with her, stay after work with her, visit her in the hospital. Much as I love my work, staying in stillness with a dying resident had been difficult and scary for me. No longer, thanks to my teacher.

* * *

from Ingrid, CNA...

We make these connections. Dave is a very nice person, always smiling. He no longer can remember my name, but he knows it is me, the person who takes care of him. His eyes tell me he feels safe.

* * *

from Merle, Housekeeper...

I visit Joan almost every day, even when I work on a different floor. I like her. She seems shy. Joan tells me, "The first time I saw you I knew I could trust you and talk to you." We talk about her life, her family and I can tell she feels better afterward.

* * *

from Beverley, CNA...

Thelma fought a lot. She'd punch, kick, you name it. I got so attached to her. She loved her husband. If you talked to Thelma about her man, all the fighting stopped. The day she died was like any other day. I gave her care in the morning, same fighting spirit. Later, we were sitting and talking and Thelma was gone. I got so close to her.

* * *

from Catherine, CNA...

Betty is 107 years old. She is a tiny little lady with a great spirit. Betty could not walk when she was admitted. She worked and worked and one day, I'll never forget it, I heard my name yelled from down the hall and it was Betty, walking. She just really touched my heart.

* * *

from Marilyn, CNA...

We'd never had a resident in Jerome's condition. He was approximately 40 years old at the time of his admission. His stay in the nursing home included intensive rehabilitation. Three years later Jerome was discharged home. That was almost three years ago.

It doesn't end there, oh no, I'm still in Jerome's life and he's still in mine. We talk often by phone and I see him every now and then. We bonded, became friends. I have a special love for him and his family. I saw him recently at his mother's funeral. She had been a resident of ours after Jerome. As his mom was being discharged home she said to me, "Marilyn, I know I'm dying. Please be there for Jerome." I visited her at their home. Jerome called me the day she passed. We cried together. I have a special love for them.

* * *

from Aeon, CNA…

I cannot give you her first name because I always refer to her as Mother. She reminds me of my great-aunt. Mother is just a wonderful woman. Mother calls me her son, tells me she misses me when I'm off and she's happy when I'm on duty. If I'm off and she refuses to eat, the staff tell her, "Your son Aeon says you should eat." And Mother eats.

* * *

from Miletta, CNA…

I have been taking care of Edwina for over eleven years, seen her through good times and bad. Whenever Edwina comes home from the hospital, all the staff tell me, "Your baby is back," because they know I love her. And no matter which assignment she returns to, everyone knows I'll be taking care of Edwina.

I've nursed her from one stage to the next, from walking and feeding herself to a wheelchair and me feeding her. I would like to be here when Edwina passes. I would want our final moment together, to wash and wrap her. If I'm not here, it will be a loss for me. I will feel like I should have been here, like maybe if I was she wouldn't have passed.

* * *

from Ann Margaret, CNA…

They are all special. When I am home, I think of them. When I vacation overseas, I call to find out about them. They're all special to me.

* * *

from Carmen, Nurse…

Regina was a terror. She was a fighter. Only in her late 60s, Regina required total care and didn't feel good about that. So she took her anger out on me. It's part of the job. We developed trust and got so close, though she remained challenging. When she passed, I felt it, but for her, she was at peace. I admired her.

* * *

from Debbie, CNA…

Marilyn is the mouthpiece for the floor. Everybody loves Marilyn. We would sit and talk about her days as a schoolteacher. Marilyn loved those kids. I took care of her for five years before I transferred a year ago. Every day I come to work early and start my day on my old floor visiting my residents. I miss them greatly, even as I am enjoying getting to know my new residents. I like to see them all happy.

* * *

from Barima, Nurse...

Ida was quite a nice woman. I became very close to her. She was very motherly. Gave good advice. When she passed, I was so touched. I won't forget Ida.

* * *

from Claritha, PTA...

Wendy was combative. When she first arrived she refused to exercise. I kept going back and eventually we bonded. "You all treated me the way I needed, you loved me." Wendy was amazing. It's years later and when we see each other she tells me, "I still remember when you walked me."

* * *

from Bernadette, Therapeutic Recreation Leader...

When I would arrive at Joanne's room to invite her to recreation programming she would always respond, "I have to clean the house first, then I'll join you." She said it with this aristocratic accent as though a lady of leisure. Joanne was the first resident I worked with who died. She taught me a lot. Like don't take people or time for granted. Stay in the moment. Joanne helped me to appreciate my time with my residents.

* * *

from Stella, Nurse...

Darla was the boss. Nobody was allowed to sit by her room. She would tell me where to park my medication cart and call me, "The Drug Dealer." If Darla saw other residents acting out or not eating or refusing medication, she would tell them, "They are here to take care of us, we must do as they ask us." Darla was the boss. I miss her.

* * *

from Cheryl, Nurse...

Jonathan, or Boobi, as he wanted me to call him, was a trip. I asked the doctor to speak with him one day because Boobi was refusing to take his medication. The doctor explained, "You need to take this medication to stay alive. Everyday you take it you will live a little longer." And Boobi spat the pills right at the doctor. Boobi told me, "Shorty, you're having a baby." Told me before I even knew. We were that close. The morning of the day he died, Boobi told me he was tired. We spoke about how he had a good life and he said, "I'm ready." His family came to visit at 4:30p.m. and twenty minutes later Boobi said to me and his family, "Excuse me," and he passed. I never cried so much in my entire life.

* * *

from Lilly, CNA...

We just connected. Lucy isn't easy to get along with. She likes me and I like her. Lucy would say, "All my life a lot of people don't like me." But I believe when you love someone, that's it, you take them as they are. I love Lucy.

* * *

from Leo, Housekeeper...

I know Rob for one year now. Every time I pass his room when he is inside, he yells, "Leo, hi." He likes to talk about when he was a soldier. We speak while I clean his room. I like Rob. We have a nice connection.

* * *

from Dennis, CNA...

When you do this work you have to put your heart into it. Edgar and me, we were pretty good together. I took care of him for eight months until three weeks ago when he transferred to another unit. He comes back to see me every day I work. When he had to make a serious medical decision, he said, "We need to talk, man to man." We're here to help people. 'Cause you never know, could be your family, could be me.

* * *

from Fidelma, Administrator...

This is going back to the late '70s. Laura just had a wonderful, wonderful spirit. We were preparing to celebrate her 100th birthday and she gave me the dress she wanted to wear. I was bringing it to work, from having it dry cleaned, on a rainy day. I dropped the dress and it was filthy all over again. We laughed. All these years and Laura stays on my mind. She touched my heart.

* * *

from Maureen, COTA...

Lizzy was the queen of the nursing home. A resident for eight years, Lizzy chose to stay in her bed for the last six years. So everyone went to Lizzy. I visited her every day I worked. You went to Lizzy for gossip and advice. The back of her room door was completely covered with pictures of her family and our staff members' children. She loved to look at those pictures.

One of our nurses called me at home one weekend. Lizzy was dying. I came and spent most of the day with her. She died the next day. Sixty staff members attended her funeral. Lizzy loved her aides. She used to say, "I wouldn't do this job for a million dollars and these girls do it with such devotion."

* * *

from Mavis, CNA...

I adopted Wanda. She spoke little English and I speak little Spanish but we worked it out. Wanda had this beautiful head of hair. I would buy all kinds of hair products and wash and set her hair how she liked it. When I changed units Wanda wouldn't cooperate. The staff would call me and she and I would come to some agreement. She is no longer living where I work, but I still go and visit her and I never miss her birthday.

* * *

from Stacey, Nurse...

When Charles was admitted he was comatose and we were told he was expected to live two weeks. His family came and said their goodbyes. It was so sad. We kept him comfortable, talked to him while we gave him care, but there was no response. Charles lay with his eyes closed in silence. Until one morning when he answered me. He scared me to death. It was so exciting, then nothing. Then a few days later a few more words, followed by conversation. Today, he eats by mouth, curses like a sailor and can be very demanding. And we celebrate all of him everyday. Every time I see him it's like wow, this is why I do this work!

* * *

from Anthony, Housekeeper...

Brad is not easy. Some days he is Brad, others, Freddy Krueger. I like him for who he is. Just knowing Brad and talking with him makes my day good. His fighting spirit is his persona. It's what keeps him strong. He's a good guy.

* * *

from Megan, CNA...

I only took care of Esther for four months and that was two years ago. Still, I think of her often. She was only 21 years old, same age as my daughters. I fell in love with her and tried to encourage her, you know, lift her spirits. On my break time we would sit and talk about boys. Esther really touched me.

* * *

from Noreen, CNA...

For ten years I took care of Joseph. I was drawn to him. His only family, his sister, lives in Florida. He became my family.

We get so close to our residents. One year ago, I transferred to another unit. I still visit Joseph every other day and his sister and I have long talks on the phone. I miss him.

* * *

from Angie, CNA...

Lucille's appearance is very important to her. We style her hair, put makeup on and get her dressed for the day. Then Lucille tells me, "We must take a walk now," and she parades up and down the unit. One day she was sad as we talked about her deceased daughter. I said to her, "I know I can't replace your daughter, but I'll be here for you to talk with." Lucille perked up and said, "You know, that's a great idea." I enjoy seeing my residents happy.

* * *

from Joy, CNA...

No matter how I tried, I didn't feel I was making Carmen happy. We had so much in common and still we couldn't hit it off. We take care of people who can't take care of themselves. It's our job to make them happy, or at least happier. I was disappointed with myself, but I continued trying. It took Carmen and me three months to find each other, but we did it. I felt so much better coming to work. Then, one month ago, she transferred to another unit. Now we miss each other. Funny, huh? I go see her a couple times a week. Carmen smiles when she sees me and we talk for a while.

* * *

from Denfield, Dietary Aide...

Oh, Veronica, she became my best friend here. We overcame difficulties to get where we are today. Veronica always had to be served first, even if she was last to come into the dining room. She would scream if I served anyone before her. One day we sat and talked for a while. It was the start of our getting close. Veronica has a greater appreciation for other people now, she's kinder. I like to think our relationship has something to do with her new outlook. She is my friend.

* * *

from Kenia, CNA...

Oh, I want to tell you about Anne. She wants to be first always, even if she is last to arrive. Anne would get so upset if someone else got cared for before her. It was really becoming a problem if I went to her room later in the morning. I was wondering why this was such an issue for her, so I went to Anne's room to talk about it with her. She told me she had many brothers, but she was the only girl so she always went first. Then as an adult, Anne had only one child so that child went first. So now I almost always do Anne first. And she waits patiently when I cannot.

* * *

from Gwen, CNA...

Every time I see the room number for Helen's room I think of her. Every day. I took care of Helen for four years. That was three years ago. I just love her. Spent my break time talking in her room each evening. I truly miss her.

* * *

from Cynthia, CNA....

We were a threesome, Minnie, Bernadette and me. They were roommates and best friends. The two of them understood each other. It was really warm to watch. I would get them ready for the day, makeup and costume jewelry I'd bring from home. Then we'd sing and dance together. They were beautiful together.

* * *

from Charles, CNA...

Here's a blessing. Carol is 105 years old. She knows me since I'm born. We lived in the same building. Carol would tell my mom if she saw me misbehaving. Still calls me, "Little Fat Charlie." I'm glad she's with me. I have the opportunity to return the favor of her caring for me by taking care of her.

* * *

from Mattie, Nurse...

Nicholas was in his 30s and cognitively impaired, yet he taught me so much. Like never underestimate anyone. He was 6'4" and had this little, little voice. Nicholas lived with his mom and wanted to go home. Problem was, his mom was suddenly too sick to take care of him. So Nicholas threatened to go on a hunger and shower strike. "I'll get skinny and stinky," he told me. You can read a chart, speak to professionals, but until you talk to the individual, you cannot know them. Thanks, Nicholas.

* * *

from Theresa, CNA...

Linda and I made a connection. She is very sweet and loving. We know each other from when Linda lived in an assisted living facility where I'd worked. Then we met up here in the nursing home. She used to come home with me and stay overnight. My children love Linda. Other residents love her. We are always getting hugs and, "I love you," from Linda. There is a resident on the unit who likes nobody and curses all the time. For some reason, Linda goes to see him and he's kind, patient with her, always friendly. That's the effect Linda has on us.

* * *

from Lorna, Laundry Aide...

You know, I've cried many times on this job. When we lose them it really touches my heart. I know Consuela for six years. Almost everyday we spend a few minutes together. She calls me her daughter. We know all there is to know about each others' family. I bring fruit from home, which she loves to eat. If my Consuela passes, I don't know how I will make out. It will break my heart. She is very dear to me.

* * *

from Laura, CNA...

I was actually just thinking of Lorraine. She comes across my heart and I wonder about her, how she's doing. We took care of her for four years. Then, five years ago, Lorraine moved to Florida to be nearer to her family. I miss her all these years later. She was in her early twenties at the time of her admission. She was very bright. On my day off I used to take her out on pass and we'd go to the library. We took the bus. Lorraine had never ridden a city bus and found it very exciting. She obtained a library card and loved to read. We had about a month's notice of Lorraine's discharge. I started missing her even before she left.

* * *

from Alisha, CNA...

Rosa is a hardball. She will scream at me, curse at me, tell me, "I don't know what you're doing here, I didn't call for you!" Then she'll ask where I was on my day off, thank me for all I do for her and tell me, "You're the only one for me." Rosa is a trip.

* * *

from Ida, Nurse...

Tina was twenty years old when she came to us. She was a challenge in many ways. She'd been on her own since the age of twelve. Her story brought tears to my eyes. I think of her often and how she allowed herself to rely on me. "C'mon ma, get real," she used to say with a smile. I love her.

* * *

from Nadine, CNA...

Jackie is amazing. She came to us a year ago at age 21. At first we didn't get much response from her. We just kept loving her, giving her attention and she came around. Now she holds you, smiles while she gives hugs. I call Jackie, "Princess," just like my daughter. They are the only two.

* * *

from Ewurakua, CNA...

Danielle is always happy to see me. She just likes me. On my days off, Danielle sleeps in her bed. But when I work, she sleeps in a chair in the hallway so she can see me coming and going. We talk, we dance. She is waiting for me at 11p.m. when I come to work. Danielle even changed my name. She calls me Clarissa and smiles. There is something about her; she's a good person.

* * *

from Joyce, Therapeutic Recreation Leader...

That would have to be William. He called me his daughter and was another dad to me. His family became my family. We would all go to dinner together—William and his wife and daughter and me and my husband and kids. Sometimes on my day off, I would go shopping with his wife. I will never forget the day his wife called from the hospital saying, "W.B. passed." There was this lump in my throat, like now.

That was eight years ago. The three of us still keep in touch by phone and get together whenever his wife and daughter come into the city. I promised myself I would never get this close to a resident. Didn't hold; you can't help it.

* * *

from Mel, Dietary Aide...

Abraham and I were tight. His sister always told me, "If something happens to me, look out, Abraham's gonna change." Man, did she know her brother! Abraham's sister passed and there was nobody else to visit him. All of a sudden he's calling me names and cursing me. Then he tells me, "Mel, I'm only kidding. I just need to keep going." Abraham touched my heart. I told him, "Whatever you need, I'm there for you."

* * *

from Diane, Therapeutic Recreation Leader...

Can I tell you about Alice? We all adored her. She died within the past year and was a challenge for the entire length of her stay.

"I want to go home," was Alice's mantra. Only there was no other home. I never saw a visitor in all her years here. Recreation staff would take Alice to their homes for the holidays—Easter, Thanksgiving, Christmas. Alice would ask to use the ladies room and God bless the person in that house who would use it next: feces all over the walls, floor, and fixtures. For many years Recreation staff brought her to their homes for many holidays. We loved her. Nobody saw the behavior; we just saw Alice.

* * *

from Tina, CNA...

Shirley loves the way I do her hair. For three years we have this bond. She is very special to me.

* * *

from Cassy, CNA...

Paulette always remembered my name. She loved to talk and was a very nice person. What I remember most was how funny she could be. Paulette never forgot her bath days. Up at 5a.m., I would be greeted at 7a.m. with a smile and, "I've been waiting for two hours for my bath." I was here when she passed away. We got so close. There is so much I remember about them.

* * *

from Karmala, Nurse...

I've known Walter for three years. It gives me so much joy to think about how much he has grown. I look forward to seeing him every day. Walter is transferring to another unit. We've spoken. He knows I'm here for him to talk to and I know I'll see him throughout the facility. But it won't be the same. I'll miss him and the chance to make him smile.

* * *

from Marva, CNA...

What a bond Bob and I have. He loves my attention. We would send another CNA to check on him and everything would be fine. Then I'd go in and this is wrong and they never did that for him and we need to do this. He'd have a list for me. I would laugh and talk with him. It really gives me pleasure to take care of our residents.

* * *

from Yvonne, Patient Representative...

Robert has been with us for 15 years. He was married for 65 years. A number of years ago they lost their son. Robert lost his wife one month ago. It is so sad.

One day Robert came to my office to talk. We do that often. He just broke down and sobbed for 25 minutes. Then he said, "When I go out there, you tell them I'm OK. I'm going to show the young people how to survive." I told Robert he is loved by many. We talked about how alone his wife would have been if he'd died first. I told him, "God doesn't make mistakes. You're a strong person with much to teach many." I opened my office door. Robert wheeled into the hallway and loudly started complaining about this and that. He had his public persona intact.

* * *

from Margaret, Secretary...

Sally just took to me. I don't get a lot of opportunity to interact with the residents, but I go to each unit to deliver certain paperwork. Sally was by the elevator almost every time I arrived to her floor. She would try to get on the elevator to leave the unit and I would redirect her. "I know what you're doing," she would yell. But somehow we took to each other. Sally would see me from across a room and come over to me and say, "I want you to do something with me." She just took to me.

* * *

from Gloria, Nurse...

Alice was one of the earliest African-American residents admitted to our facility. She was a woman of many, many parts, one day telling you off and the next sharing stories of her relatives or swapping recipes. All Alice wanted was to go home. And, of course, she had no home other than the nursing home. Her family were all in South Carolina. And so we went. I escorted Alice home. It was the trip of a lifetime. We flew, stayed in a hotel and visited her sister and other relatives. Leave it to Alice, she spoke to no one. I can never, never, never forget Alice.

* * *

from Selina, CNA...

There is just something about Catherine that has touched me. I love her. She is a real lady. We talk; she confides in me. I love her.

* * *

from Ralph, Nurse...

Michael and I were working together, we really were. Some days he would recognize me and greet me with, "Hey buddy." Others , I would be met with, "Are you here to fight me?" But we were coming along. About two weeks ago Michael transferred to another unit. Don't get me wrong, I know the transfer was in his best interest. It's just, I miss the guy.

* * *

from Trixie, Nurse…

Myrna came to us for short-term rehab and hoped, no, planned, to go home. It wasn't to be. She just didn't get well enough to where her family could provide the necessary care. Myrna was so disappointed. For a while she wouldn't speak. The staff just kept loving her, closed the trust gap. And she settled in beautifully. Myrna is very special to us.

* * *

from Hazel, CNA…

Lola was very sick when she came to us about two years ago. She is a very nice, young lady in her thirties. For the past year since she discharged home, we have kept in touch. Just yesterday she came by the nursing home and found me. Lola had a difficult early life. Today she is on her own and going to school. She brings me her grade reports and cries when she tells me how encouraging I am to her. Lola is such a nice person and I am glad to do it.

* * *

from Emily, CNA…

There is someone I am missing terribly right now. I took care of Pam for seven months. She spent most of each shift I worked right by my side. Pam would go with me and wait while I gave care to my other residents. She would help in the dining room, handing out silverware. When I came off the elevator to start my shift, Pam would be sitting, waiting for me. One week ago she transferred to another unit. I took her over, we were crying together the whole way. I would love to go see her, but I know she needs time to adjust. I love her. I'll know when it's right and I can't wait to see her.

* * *

from Betty, CNA…

When Mary first was admitted she was very withdrawn. She wouldn't speak and no one was allowed to touch her. Slowly she came out of her shell. Now she eats her meals with her dining room buddies. I really don't know how we connected. Mary is so happy to see me every day. "Good morning Betty," she'd say with a big smile. On my return from jury duty I was greeted with, "You're back, you're home now. I missed you." It makes me feel good.

* * *

from Meggy, CNA…

Oh, Carlos. I only worked here for three months when he died, and I never was assigned to take care of him. He was so sweet. I got to know him by translating between him and my co-workers. Carlos only spoke Spanish. He was 105 years old, did almost everything for himself until the day he passed. Every day Carlos would walk past the picture of St. Elizabeth and touch it and make the sign of the cross. He would ask us to heat his milk for his cereal. He liked it warm. It's funny, the little things that stay with me. I cried so much when Carlos passed. He reminded me of my own grandfather.

* * *

from Hope, CNA…

I took care of Carolyn for four years. We became so close. Two years ago my job was transferred to another floor. I visit Carolyn almost every day. She's dying and doesn't recognize me, but I sit with her. It's so hard.

* * *

from Ebeneezer, Housekeeper…

Timothy was a distinguished gentleman. He would tell me stories about how he met with diplomats from all over the world. He spoke with pride. If I was cleaning his room and someone came on the TV news that he knew, he would say, "Ebeneezer, I knew him." And he would tell me the story. A real gentleman.

* * *

from Nadine, Therapeutic Recreation Leader…

My grandfather passed away and Jerome told me, "I will be your grandfather now." And he was. Jerome would make me laugh, give me advice, check to see I was doing well in school, you know, things a grandfather does for you. He died on my 20th birthday. I just burst out crying. Jerome was close to my heart. He was my booboo.

* * *

from Nathan, Dietary Aide…

Carla was sweet. She was like a grandmother to me. When I would bring her tray, she would kiss me on the cheek and we'd ask about each other's day. I told her my wife was expecting a baby. Carla told me, "I hope to see the baby before I die." She always seemed so comfortable speaking about her death. I was so happy to bring my daughter to see Carla. She held her and just smiled . When Carla passed, it was like losing my grandmother. That's what happens when you get close.

* * *

from Catherine, Therapeutic Recreation Leader...

There is a gentleman on the floor right now who gets to me. He has really touched me. Daniel expresses his affection through sarcasm. It's his way of not letting himself become too vulnerable. I'll ask him if I'm his favorite girl and he'll answer gruffly, "No, and you never will be." On July 4th, I baked him a cake—white frosting, blueberries in the top left corner, strawberries across the cake. I asked him how it tasted. He looked at me with disdain and said, "It was from hunger." Then he proceeded to eat the whole thing. I feel such a closeness to him, it's unbelievable.

* * *

from Cynthia, CNA...

We have been caring for Sheila for nine years. She is a retired Army Sergeant. Sheila carried over two things from the army: she was always singing army songs and she remained very regimented. Things had to be just so with Sheila. When she arrived at the dining room, the table needed to be tidy and there better be quiet during the meal. As Sheila declined over the last year, she stopped singing her songs. We miss those songs. I enjoy taking care of my residents and I am happy just to know Sheila.

* * *

from Aley, Nurse...

Gary was in an accident at age 28 which left him seriously injured. Now, at age 43, he was dying. He had a remarkable relationship with his brother. Through it all his brother stood by him. He took care of him at home for as long as possible and visited daily at the nursing home. Every penny of Gary's accident award was spent on Gary. The money remaining after Gary passed away, his brother donated all of it to charities. Gary was always worried about what would happen to his brother when he died. They truly loved one another.

* * *

from Naomi, CNA...

Her name was Asia. I was just taken with her. She was fresh, liked to push your buttons, would roll her eyes, then laugh. I loved her and I know she loved me. It's hard to talk about her without crying. I miss her.

* * *

from Juliette, Nurse...

Forrest is 82 years old and very confused. He is very combative, wanders and can be extremely difficult. I tell myself there must be a way to get through to him. At times, when I find him having wandered on the unit, he lets me sit beside him. We're not talking, but we're there in the moment, together.

* * *

from Audrey, CNA…

I have taken care of Millie for two years. For some reason, I just took to her. And it's not because she's easy. When I give her care, she screams, kicks, spits. She's a tiny lady but she hurts. When I take her out of her room Millie tells anybody and everybody, "She's my baby, yeah, she's my baby." I love Millie.

* * *

from Maxine, CNA…

Kathy and I developed this relationship where we had a signal. When Kathy was ready for bed she would just come to her door and call like an owl, "Ooo, ooo." Everyone knew. If I didn't hear her, a co-worker would find me and tell me, "Kathy's calling." I didn't know this would hurt so much. Kathy got sick and needed to transfer to another unit. Kathy, her daughter and I had a good cry over that. One of us visited the other every day I worked. Then Kathy got sicker. At the end she told me, "I'm going to go." I just held her hand. And then I cried some more.

* * *

from Berenthia, CNA…

Lisa was a challenge. Somehow we made a connection despite her confusion. Every day she would come with me to each room and wait for me while I was inside giving care to my resident. Lisa was not on my assignment. If her aide didn't get her up first (you can't get the same person up first all the time), Lisa would find me when she was out of bed and say, "You started without me." At the end of each shift I would go to see her and she would always kiss me goodnight. I loved her and she loved me. I miss her.

* * *

from Eulean, Housekeeper...

Chris was from my country. I think that is where the trust started. We would talk every day while I cleaned his room. He would open up to me. We were very close. I always brought him stuff from back home when I returned from vacation. Chris was my best friend for three years. I was so shocked when he passed. He's gone five years and I still miss him and think of him often.

* * *

from Leslie, Social Worker...

Jean talks constantly, and always in the third person: "Jean has to go to the bathroom, Jean wants to go to bed now." I just enjoy talking with her. She is so animated. Like when I am talking about her, stories from her past, her eyes open wide with wonder and she asks, "How do you know so much about me?" I answer, "We speak almost daily and you tell me all about yourself," to which Jean replies, "Oh, that's nice." I feel real close to her.

* * *

from Bernadine, CNA...

Ring the bell, ring the bell, all Catherine did was ring the bell. Coffee, sugar, bathroom, just talk, anything and everything and nothing. By the time I leave the room, the bell is ringing again. Catherine died a month ago and I miss her terribly. It's quiet here without her.

* * *

from Agatha, CNA...

Joe's a comical womanizer. One day he announced to his sons, "We're married and there's nothing you can do about it", right out of the blue. I don't know where he got that one from. They are all special in their own way. There is so much joy in taking care of them.

* * *

from Wendy, Nurse...

I met Sheila as a student intern twenty three years ago and a bond developed immediately. Through the years, we have seen each other almost daily. My wedding picture is in her room, at Sheila's request. Not a birthday goes by without a card. Even my son gets a card each year. Sheila is truly close to my heart.

* * *

from Daisy, CNA...

Johnny was a father figure. He would introduce me to others as, "my Nurse Daisy." We got along so well. Johnny was a sensitive person. If he saw a sad story on TV, he'd be crying in his room. He loved for me to rub his head to calm him down, put him at peace. After caring for Johnny for a year, he transferred. I got so attached, it's like part of me is missing.

* * *

from Patricia, CNA...

Franklin was such a remarkable man. We were so attached. If he was on another assignment, all the CNA or Nurse had to do was say my name and Franklin would cooperate. His daughter and I each had three kids and Franklin kind of adopted mine. He would ask about them and give me advice as if they were his "grands." I visited him in the hospital every day near his end. Franklin is gone five years and he stays on my mind and in my heart.

* * *

from Millicent, CNA...

Cynthia wanders for the two years I know her. Rarely stays in one place. When I take her to her room in the middle of the night, she rubs and kisses my hand while we walk. Cynthia gives me a big smile and promises to stay in bed. By the time I'm up the hall, she's up again. I am so close to her. She could be my mother. They are all part of my family.

* * *

from Lorraine, Unit Clerk...

One day the ambulance attendants were bringing Benjamin back to the unit from the hospital. Benjamin asked,

"Where are we?," to which the attendants responded, "You're home." "This is not my home, let's get out of here." Then Benjamin raised his head, saw me, and said, "Oh yeah, there's the lady that does all the paperwork. I am home." We laughed. Benjamin would spend the better part of my work day sitting beside me talking about anything and everything.

* * *

from Alberta, Housekeeper…

Betty Anne is 101 years old. She has lived here for one year. What I appreciate is her strength as a woman and the advice she gives me. "Hold your head high, take care of the children and stay with your man." That is her approach to life. She is a good person, always willing to talk.

* * *

from Eileen, CNA…

I have been taking care of Yvette for two years. She has no family. I was immediately drawn to her as a grandmother. When I arrive for work and go to her room, I am greeted with, "I'm so glad you're here. I know you know me.'" I am very close with Yvette.

* * *

from Rose, CNA…

Kevin was like a father to me. I was so attached to him. I started every day I worked with Kevin, whether he was on my assignment or not. Nice man. He would tell me, "Honey, you're a hell of a woman." I would buy him Pepsi and chips and we would talk. He died while I was on vacation. I feel so sad when I think of losing him.

* * *

from Andree, Nurse...

I attended Catholic school as a young girl. Lola was a teacher during her work years. We would sit and talk—on my break time, before and after my shifts. I would tell her, "You served a great deal of people and gave much to the world. Now we are here to take care of you." We would pray together. Lola would tell me, "I love you. Can I hug you?" And hug we would.

* * *

from Stella, Therapeutic Recreation Leader...

Oh, Leslie, she taught me so much, helped me with other residents. Leslie didn't socialize much, kept to herself mostly. We were going to see "Opera in the Park" on the lawn in Central Park. I invited her and she agreed to join us. Leslie knew all the words, had a beautiful voice and sang the night away. She taught me to get in touch with what the residents are in touch with. Leslie died soon after the trip and I was so glad to have seen her so happy.

* * *

from Evelyn, CNA...

I have been caring for Lee for four years. She is 97 years old and in failing health. When Lee first got here she'd fight and call names each time I'd go to give care. It was hard because it hurt me, what she was saying, and because I knew how hard it was for Lee to accept needing to be here. We've gotten so close, like she's my mother. When I think of the future without her, it hurts. I will miss her.

* * *

from Dekeya, Nurse...

Juana had been a CNA. She was so quiet, wouldn't ask for help. "You can come in any time and we can talk," she would say. That's how our connection began. I'd make multiple visits to make sure that Juana was okay and we'd talk. At some point I started visiting with her right before my shift started. I admired her, took care of her for two years. When we lost her, it was hard.

* * *

from Marina, CNA...

I took care of Evelyn for three years. That was six years ago. Her improvement is a miracle: from bed-bound and not eating to independent and a volunteer. Evelyn and I visit each other weekly. She loves to share the activities of her week. I encourage her and listen. When I was recovering from a car accident, Evelyn called me every week until I came back to work.

* * *

from Loletta, CNA...

We were very, very close. We grew to love each other. I would mend her clothes at home. Joyce called me every week when I was home with a back injury. We said prayers together before she went to bed each night. I will never forget Joyce.

* * *

from Catherine, Nurse…

Phyllis was a resident here for about four months. I have never met a braver person. I admired her courage. Phyllis was terminally ill but was terminally positive as well. She was encouraging to everyone, especially her roommate. I will never forget her courage.

* * *

from Sylvia, CNA…

I call Margaret, "Mom", and she calls me, "Daughter". Margaret makes us all laugh. She is a storyteller—some true, some not, all pretty funny. Every now and then Margaret orders in lunch from a local restaurant. She calls for me to help her set up and tells me, "Sit down, I ordered enough for my daughter, too." I always remember her birthday and we exchange cards at Christmas. We are family.

* * *

from Melva, CNA…

A pleasant woman was Amy. At 93 years old she was a sweet old soul. When I came to her early each morning to get her ready for the day, she would recite her prayer card for the day to me. Amy was Jamaican, like myself. We have a saying that was a favorite of hers—one woncoppo full basket. It means you won't achieve it all in one day, you must keep working. I wasn't ready when we lost her; none of us were.

* * *

from Karen, Housekeeper...

Let me put it this way. Mary didn't quite receive me in at first. It took me some time to break the ice. I kept going back, talking to her while I cleaned her room. I wanted to put her at ease. Now we have a relationship. We put on music and I tell her, "Let's dance." She just laughs while I dance for her.

* * *

from Edwina, CNA...

I took care of Debbie for ten years. She was so nice, always a good attitude. In the morning, I'd ask her how she was and Debbie would always answer, "Good Lord woke me up this morning, I'm fine." One day Recreation had a live band playing music. Debbie attended and really enjoyed herself. Later in the day she was crying and I offered support. She said her husband had been a band player. She touched my heart and we cried together. For me she was like a mother. I miss her very much.

* * *

from Lorraine, Unit Clerk...

I got so attached to Anthony. He lived with us for three years and every day I worked I fed him lunch. I looked forward to feeding him. It was our time together. I still think of him sometimes when I go to lunch.

* * *

from Augustina, CNA...

I took care of Lydia for six years until I changed units. We are very close. I think about her all the time. She is legally blind but recognizes my voice and touches my face. I feed Lydia breakfast every morning and we talk to start each day. I am very attached to her.

* * *

from Inez, CNA...

Mae was so encouraging to all of us. She could tell if something was bothering someone and she'd ask, "What's wrong, you don't look right." Mae always reminded us that, "No matter what you're going through, somebody has it worse." She was just very encouraging. We all still talk about her.

* * *

from Aeon, CNA...

There were four men on the unit a few years back; Isaac, Robert, Charles and John. They were comfortable with me and each other. There was love. Each summer I would take them to the city for a nice seafood dinner. Then, around the holidays, we'd drive around the city looking at Christmas lights. It was our tradition.

* * *

from Gloria, Nurse...

It was my first day on the job. I was a nurse! Paul is unforgettable. He was my savior five shifts per week until I knew all 40 of my residents. I was struggling to give medications to 40 strangers and Paul saw my struggle. And so, on literally my first shift as a nurse, a resident saved me. Paul came over toward me and said, "Nurse, I know everybody here. I'll take you around." And so I had my escort for medication rounds. It was so kind of him and I told him so over the years. He is unforgettable.

* * *

from Pauline, CNA...

They're all special. The love I have for them keeps me coming here every day. My own grandmother died on Mother's Day, 1990, home in Jamaica. I wasn't there to care for her so I extend myself for those who cannot care for themselves. Somehow, I am taking care of my grandmother when I take care of and love them.

* * *

from Movell, CNA...

Augustina kind of chose me. She calls me her daughter and gives me a motherly feel. Augustina reminds me so much of my grandmother, when she was alive. I used to buy her things-clothing, lipstick, make-up. She loved getting all fancied up. Augustina transferred to the 3rd floor about a year ago. I visit her and she always greets me with, "How is my daughter?." We hug and kiss. She tells me, "You are my special person; I will always remember you." And I will never forget her.

* * *

from Jennifer, Nurse...

Alisha came to us near death. We took care of her for one and a half years. Her recovery was a great miracle. I am very proud of what we were able to do for her. About nine months ago Alisha went home to Trinidad. Eating and talking again.

I've spoken to her twice since she went home. She will remain on my mind, maybe forever.

* * *

from Najuma, Therapeutic Recreation Leader...

Marva was feisty. She liked to talk tough, but underneath she was really soft. I miss her. She was a businesswoman and spoke as if still the boss and then some. Marva's way of requesting assistance would go something like, "This is what I need, this is how it is to be done, and now, or I'll throw you out the window." Or if she needed help from a CNA, she would say, "Honey, honey, where are the girls? Tell the girls I need them," always putting herself above you. She was a trip.

* * *

from Marva, CNA...

I used to sit and talk with Dora every night. We became good friends. She would tell me, "I wish you were related to me." Even when Dora wasn't on my assignment, I took care of her. She would get scared, feeling like she was going to die. We would pray together and that would give her comfort. We lost Dora two years ago. I still think of her often.

* * *

from Irma, Nursing Secretary...

My mom was a resident here for a year. Mom passed away in 1993. Julie lives on the same floor my mom did. That's how we got to know each other. Everyday since, we speak. For the past thirteen years, Julie comes down to the Nursing office and starts me on my day. Every day. We talk about family, current events, anything. Then Julie tells me, "Go back to work." It makes me feel good to make her feel good. She leaves happy and that makes me happy.

* * *

from Paulette, CNA...

Penny has been with us for two months. When she first arrived it was hard to please her. Penny was restless, frustrated at her situation and scared. We gave her the attention she needed and she gained assurance and confidence. That enabled her to make physical progress. Penny amazes me. I feel so good having something to do with how well she has improved.

* * *

from Samonie, Nurse...

Sharon, it has to be. Sharon is a woman I took care of at my previous job. I see her every few months, ever since I left seven years ago. In between visits her nurse calls and puts Sharon on the phone and we chat. When I get to the home she greets me with, "Samonie, you came,'" and a hug and kiss. Periodically, when Sharon gets in one of her moods and refuses to shower, the staff calls for help. I stop on my way to work and give her a shower. She is still my resident.

* * *

from Icina, CNA...

Inez is so close to me she calls me, "my Icina." Every day I visit with her, even when she is not on my assignment. The first Sunday after Inez was admitted—this is ten years ago—was Easter. We got her all dressed up for church service. And ever since, Inez wants to dress just as formally each Sunday to go to church. I enjoy taking care of my residents.

* * *

from Sheldon, Nurse...

Mark is 96 years old and sharp as a tack. If I'm off one night, when I get to the floor the next afternoon, there's Mark to greet me and tell me he missed me. He has a doctor's order for a neck rub. Mark tells me all the time nobody rubs his neck like I do. One night he told me, "Oh honey, that's good; even the baby maker is getting excited." I came back to work last night after three days off. There was Mark with, "Well, hello there." It makes my day.

* * *

from Carol, Unit Clerk...

Billy referred to me as his daughter. He called me Carol and I called him Pop. His daughter and I have the same name. When she'd call the unit and I answered the phone, she always said, "Hi, it's Carol," and I'd say, "Hi, it's the other Carol," and we'd laugh. If Billy needed help with anything, he would say to a staff member, "Tell my daughter I need to see her," and I would go and help him.

* * *

from Alsea, Nurse...

We took care of Peggy and Irma for about two years. That was thirteen years ago. Talk about a love/hate relationship.

Peggy and Irma were roommates and they were inseparable. Called each other "sister." And they fought like sisters, too. But don't try to come between them, don't dare! On my break time the three of us would sit on the patio and talk. I loved them so much.

* * *

from Cliff, Social Worker...

We lost Elisa three months ago, after caring for her for two years. There is such a thick sense of loss for everyone on the unit, residents and staff alike. Elisa had such a spirit. She brought life to all that lived or worked here. Elisa would be dancing one minute and telling you off the next. At one hundred years old, Elisa's energy was good for the staff. I would say she helped us do the work we do. We all miss her greatly.

* * *

from Shawanna, CNA...

Every time I go into this certain room I think of Diane. When she arrived, Diane couldn't speak and required total care. I would talk to her the whole time I would be giving her care. Then one day, after a few months, Diane spoke. It was beautiful. Diane said, "I'm surprised you put up with me, talking to me, taking care of me like I was your mom. I kept thinking, *You'll give up on me*, but you didn't." Watching her walk out of here was a great feeling. But I miss her.

* * *

from Sister Sheila, Director of Pastoral Care...

Joan was an open, free spirit. She was a beautiful soul. Ninety-four when she arrived and 101 when she left us. Joan was a special lady. She attended almost all of the social activities, danced, played accordion and knitted almost until the day she died. Joan chose all the music for her funeral. She was like a mother to me. I just knew I was going to miss her.

* * *

from Lisa, CNA...

We just connected. She fell in love with me, and was a second mother to me. We became family, we were very close. Camilla died three days after my mom. I took care of her every day for almost three years. That was six years ago. Her daughter Concetta and I helped each other. We grieved together. Concetta and I still write to each other and we each leave flowers at our mom's gravesites. They are buried just a section apart in the same cemetery. We miss our moms.

* * *

from Darryl, Dietary Aide...

Nadine is the sweetest. Great smile, good talker. The nurses couldn't get Nadine to eat. Nobody could. One day in the dining room, the nurse said to me, "We're going to fire you if Nadine doesn't eat, we don't need you." Nadine called me over and said, "I'll eat, if they're going to fire you. I want to keep you around." And so she eats.

* * *

from Josephine, CNA...

There is something special about her. Theresa is confused and gets quite agitated. Concerns about how she will pay her bills or get to bed at night can overwhelm her. I tell her, "I'm here to take care of you. I'm responsible for you. That's why I work here, to take care of you. You are OK." Theresa holds my hand and smiles. The last thing she tells me each night is, "God bless you."

* * *

from Monica, Therapeutic Recreation Leader...

Kay was a tomboy, a street girl even. At eight years old she was playing on rooftops. We didn't always get along. She can be judgmental of other residents, so we would argue. Kay would always win. We kind of won each other over and began loving each other. Now she sees me and greets me with a big smile, asking, "So, you want to talk?"

* * *

from Marjorie, CNA...

Emily was terminally ill. Still, she greeted me with a smile every day. We just clicked. I looked forward to seeing her. In her final days she would tell me, "Once you're here, I'm comfortable." That carries me to this day. When she passed, I knew it was best for Emily, but for me, I miss her. So every day on the job, if I can make at least one person's life better, make one person happy, then I'm happy.

LAUGHS

A smile starts on the lips
A grin spreads to the eyes
A chuckle comes from the belly
But a good laugh
Bursts forth from the soul...

Carolyn Birmingham

from Alisha, CNA…

Lois was a gem. We all called her grandma. After caring for her for eight years, we lost grandma four years ago. She took care of us as much as we did her. Grandma used to say, "You know how to get a man? You shake it up, you shake it down, but the best way to get him is put it flat on the ground." I will never forget grandma.

* * *

from Glenda, CNA…

We give them a second life. Barbara made the work easier by making you laugh. I looked forward to seeing Barbara every day. Here's typical Barbara. The nurse told me her son was on the phone from California. I brought Barbara to the nursing station and positioned her so the phone could reach her comfortably. I stepped to the side to wait, so I could return her to her room when she finished talking. After hello and some small talk, Barbara, like a lady, excused herself from the conversation and covered the mouthpiece with her palm. "Why the *!\$* are you standing there? My son wants to speak to me privately," was immediately followed by, "Hi, honey, I'm back." I cracked up. And that was Barbara.

* * *

from Edith, Dietary Aide…

Patricia has a regular visitor, almost daily, who is a Catholic nun. One day I overheard Patricia asking her friend,

"How come you don't have a husband? Don't you have a man?" Her friend blushed, rolled her eyes and answered, "Oh no, we're nuns, we don't have husbands."

* * *

from David, Dietary Aide…

I spoke to Susan nearly every day for eight years. She never called me by my name, just yelled, "Hey." This happened so often that when Susan yelled, "hey," my co-workers would turn and tell me, "David, Susan's calling you."

* * *

from Tom, Therapeutic Recreation Leader…

Juan was a plumber by trade. One night, everyone was being paged to the same unit: Housekeeping, Maintenance, Security. So I went up figuring something was up. The sight of a drenched Juan was hysterical. Having smuggled tools from a work cart, he had taken apart the water fountain.

* * *

from Bibi, CNA…

When Matilda was asked if she eats regular or diet ice cream, she replied, "I don't know, ask Bibi; she knows everything about everyone." They make me laugh. All I have to do is just touch them, an arm, a shoulder, hold a hand, and their faces light up with smiles.

* * *

from Diane, Therapeutic Recreation Leader...

Gertrude was an Italian lady and a devout Catholic. She never missed Mass. Gertrude always carried her pocketbook. One day at Catholic Service, Gertrude was receiving communion when I saw her place the Host in her pocketbook. The priest approached her and explained that the Host was meant to be eaten at that moment as part of the ceremony. Gertrude stated, "I ate it." The priest asked to see her pocketbook and attempted to open the bag. The resident pulled the bag toward her and they began to struggle. The priest was trying once again to explain the importance of the Host when Gertrude freed the pocketbook from his grasp and began hitting him on the head. This all happened within seconds. The look on the priest's face was priceless.

* * *

from Zonelyn, Rehab Transporter...

Brenda, a.k.a. the Mayor or the Governor, makes rounds daily, walking with her walker, going floor to floor. A past president of the Resident Council, Brenda greets you with a threatening, "Do you know who I am?" as she makes her way through the building. She has a great sense of humor and loves to engage the staff all over the facility.

* * *

from Tina, CNA...

I took care of Jennifer for three years, ages 102, 103 and 104. And for those three years, every time I asked her how old she was, Jennifer replied, "45."

* * *

from Wilhelmina, Nurse…

George was a real gentleman. He wore a suit and necktie every day. George used to say he didn't marry because a wife is expensive. We would sit in the dining room and talk and he would say we were out on a date. I knew him for three years, truly a gentleman.

* * *

from Silleana, CNA…

We all called her Mama. That's all I knew her by. Most jealous resident I ever cared for. Mama was funny. She would see me go to give care to her roommate and just start yelling, "Why does she call you? What are you doing over there? I need you here with me!" This was after I'd already taken care of Mama. I would sit with her for a while to calm her, but I had to take care of other residents, too.

* * *

from Thresyamma, Nurse…

They communicate in different ways. Jeannie wandered all over the unit. She would enter residents' rooms at times. One day she was taking clothing from someone's dresser. I returned the items, placing them back in the drawers, and returned to the nursing station. Jeannie was walking away from the station with my Doctor communication book. I was able to retrieve it with no fuss. The next thing I see is a linen cart being pushed the length of the unit. It was Jeannie dropping the cart at the nursing station. I think she was saying, "If I can't take it from you, I'll bring it to you."

* * *

from Esther, CNA…

Hope and my husband have the same birthday. They also share two traits; they both love attention (and know how to get it) and they both can read my mood. One day, as I entered Hope's room, I said, "Good morning, Mrs. Smith." To which Hope replied, "What's wrong? What happened last night?" And I was feeling down that morning and it touched me that she noticed. She said, "You always call me Hope, but you just called me Mrs. Smith. That's how I knew something was wrong." We laughed at how well we'd gotten to know one another.

* * *

from Patricia, CNA…

Reginald was dependable. Same story every morning: "Why you coming in here bothering me?" Each day I would try to explain that I was here to help him. "You don't have to get me up. I was in the army 30 years. I know how to get myself up. I'm not looking for a woman. I would have called you. The only way you could get me up is to get up here in the bed." All this, day after day, while he let me wash and dress him.

* * *

from Carmen, Nurse…

Todd was a tiny guy with a big crooked nose. After getting him ready for the day he asked, "Where should I go?" I said, "follow your nose; breakfast is being served." Todd responded, "If I follow my nose, I'll be going in circles all day."

* * *

from Veronica, CNA...

Gloria was 102 years old. She had been a professional seamstress and clothing remained important to her. Gloria picked out her own clothes each day. I would be making her bed or picking something up from the floor and I would feel a tug on my back. "Your blouse should cover your butt," she would say as she pulled it down around me. We would laugh together.

* * *

from Carol, Nurse...

Every day Elaine had eggs for breakfast, by request. One morning she only received one egg. She called me over, pointed to her plate and asked, "What happened to all the chickens that I only get one egg?"

* * *

from Vaslin, Nurse...

We've been caring for Elvira for five years. When she arrived, at age 100, her sons were very concerned about her food consumption. Seemed Elvira hadn't been eating well in the community. Tired of their daily questioning, Elvira took to saving her three daily menu slips and holding them up her blouse sleeve. When her sons would visit, she would whip out the menus and tell them, "Here's what I ate!"

* * *

from Diane, Therapeutic Recreation Leader...

I learn something every day here. The residents teach

us lessons in life. Like when Angela showed me not to make assumptions. She was our Resident Council Vice President and needed to run her first Council meeting. Here's when my lesson began. I presented Angela with the microphone, explaining that it would help the other residents hear her better. By the time I reached my seat in the back, Angela was addressing the group. The sight of Angela humbled me, touched my heart and I will never forget her sitting in front, eloquently leading the meeting, holding the microphone to her ear.

* * *

from Charles, CNA...

Jeff used to get me good. He'd ask, "How's your wife?" And I'd answer him "She's fine." And, laughing hysterically, Jeff would say, "I know she is."

* * *

from Patricia, CNA...

One day Jim just cracked me up. He was in bed so his doctor could examine him. With the physician on one side of the bed and me on the other, Jim whispered to me, "Every time he comes here, he wants to examine my rear. I think it's becoming a habit." We both just laughed so hard.

* * *

from Dorothy, CNA...

"Nancy was tough, on the outside. Some residents show you their soft side. Not Nancy. Her love was in her sarcasm. She would curse you like there's no tomorrow. Nancy would say, "OK, I'm old, I'm sick, my mind comes and goes, but I'm gonna give you hell 'til the bitter end." That's why I liked her. She was feisty.

* * *

from Ann, Nurse…

Larry was in his thirties. Though he never knew my name, he always recognized me by face and called me "Mama, Mama." Larry transferred from our unit about a year ago. I still visit him. He rarely spoke and when he did he used one-word sentences. One day I went to see him just before my shift started. I was still wearing my coat and hat. When I got to his room and said hello, Larry responded, "Look at you, you look like you came from the ghetto," and we laughed. It was the most he'd ever said. I can't get over him.

* * *

from Laverne, Nurse…

My staff used to call me Alberta's angel for the way I would help one resident get all dolled up. Dress, make-up, beads, lipstick and rouge, earrings and always her pocketbook. And why? Because, as Alberta would say as she exited her room for the day room, "I'm going to the club." She was a trip. Hoarded all kinds of food items. One day, walking away from lunch, her diaper looked extra-filled. Turned out to be a can of soda. "I'm going to jail. I hope the judge will go easy on me," Alberta said laughing.

* * *

from Dora, CNA...

Nicole was quiet when she first arrived. One day she was hanging up the phone as I entered her room. "Who was that? Mr. Bush?", I asked. Nicole laughed and answered, "Your hair is making you taller." The ice was broken and we have been friends ever since.

* * *

from Wilda, CNA...

Stephanie would never repeat herself if you didn't hear her the first time. She made me a better listener. I will never forget her response if you asked her to please say it again. She would roll her eyes and say, "I don't spill my cabbage twice."

* * *

from Esther, CNA...

Mr. and Mrs. C. shared a room. She was very jealous. If I came to take care of him and Mrs. C. was there, she stayed put. If she came back to the room and I was already taking care of him, she would shriek, "Aha, just as I thought, sneaked away, God knows what's going on!"

* * *

from Hyacinth, CNA...

Ben was able to take care of himself in the morning. Most days he was sitting up, washed and dressed, by the time I got to his room. But every now and then, trouble! Ben's roommate needed assistance in the morning. Every now and then, while

I took care of Glen, Ben would just scream, "I want to get up, I need help, you always help him first, nobody tends to me." Then, when I would go to help him, Ben would take care of himself. He just wanted some attention, too.

* * *

from Yvonne, Patient Representative...

I'm going back now twenty-plus years. I will never, ever forget Edith. We all called her "twinkle toes." Edith had use of only one arm and hand. She was awesome. Every morning, weather permitting, she would go outside in her wheelchair. There, using her reacher stick, she would slowly and methodically remove her shoes and socks. Then she would place bird seed on her feet and watch the birds come land on her toes and eat breakfast from her feet. Those were her babies.

* * *

from Imogene, CNA...

Ellen was a character. I was always happy to come to work just to go to her room and talk. She would curse you out with one breath and call you her friend with the next. Always grateful for all we did for her, Ellen would call you, "%^& wiper" and laugh!

* * *

from Patricia, CNA...

Once, a few years ago, a male resident asked me, "Why are you doing this work? You are so young and so pretty." I asked him if he would prefer an old ugly woman to take care of him and he answered, "I take back what I said. I never looked at it that way before."

* * *

from Jean, CNA and Miletta, CNA…

Jasmine was so funny. She had three roommates and would lay all their clothes on their beds and tell staff she was holding a clothing sale. We would tell her we had no money, to try gently to say no thank you, and she would tell us to take what we wanted and pay her when we could.

* * *

from Vaslin, Nurse…

Connie was a bubbly person, full of energy. A believer in telling the truth, she could cut to the chase with the best of them. The night of my first shift, the supervisor introduced us. Connie had inquired as to who the new face was and was told I was the new nurse. I smiled and said, "Hello." Connie smiled and said, "You don't look like you know sh——." Our relationship began that moment and I've loved her ever since.

* * *

from Joyce, Therapeutic Recreation Leader…

Ingrid was always trying to elope through the back door. We were bringing her back to the unit every day during her stay. On the day of her discharge home with her family, she refused to leave. Each time we headed toward the Main Lobby she would resist. We told her family we'd meet them outside.

Then we took Ingrid out via the back door, her favorite. She discharged home with no problem.

* * *

from Edwina, CNA...

Katie was so funny. Always knew I would laugh when giving care to Katie. One day, ready to put on her socks, I said, "Give me your foot," to which Katie replied, "If I give you my foot, what will I do?"

* * *

from Jane, CNA...

Pauline referred to me as her daughter-in-law. Introduced me to everyone as her daughter-in-law. Once introduced me that way to her son!

* * *

from Zabidea, CNA...

Bruce was so funny. He was actually a very jealous man. I always had to tell him when I would be off or he would be upset when I came back to work. Also, he didn't like me taking care of other residents. One time a resident pulled my hair and Bruce saw it happen. When his daughters came to visit, he told them, "She went and could've gotten killed."

* * *

from Diane, Therapeutic Recreation Leader...

Our owner collects antiques. Among her pieces was a gorgeous wooden antique Santa Claus. It had that worn, old weathered look and feel. Two of our residents, Earl and James, brought the statue to arts and crafts. Before anyone saw what was happening, they had the red, white, and black paint going. We had a shiny new Santa and one less antique.

* * *

from Danielle, Nurse...

Clive used to get a female visitor quite regularly. He would come to the desk and say, "We are going to my room for Bible Study and we need privacy.'" One day, shortly after "Bible Study" had begun, I heard Clive calling out my name. I ran to the room, knocked on the door and entered. Clive and his Bible Study partner were half dressed. Clive had fallen from the bed to the floor. I helped him up. Clive couldn't look me in the eye for a week.

* * *

from Regina, CNA...

Douglas is 96 years old. He is such a nice guy. His wife is deceased. When I come back from a day off, Douglas greets me with, " I miss you, do you want to come to bed with me?" We laugh. I love him. He tells me, "Be good, God loves you and I know you love me." He is special to me.

* * *

from Sharon, CNA...

Lucy was blind, but she knew me. She recognized my voice, even knew my presence. One day she told another CNA, "You're not Jonesey, you don't smell like Jonesey."

LOSSES

To every thing there is a season
And a time to every purpose
Under the heaven;
A time to be born
And a time to die...

Ecclesiastes 3:1-2

from Perpetual, CNA...

Sharon was with us for five days. I fell in love with her the first day I saw her. That happens here a lot. Sharon did not let us unpack her belongings. She always said, "I'm going home." One night when I came to work the staff said Sharon was pacing more and we should keep a close eye because she'd been saying all shift, "I'm going home." When my shift arrived, Sharon was telling the ladies from the prior shift, "If you come back and don't see me, I am saying goodbye and take care of yourself."

After pacing a while longer, Sharon put herself to bed, though she remained, as always, all dressed up. And she never woke up. "I'm going home," suddenly had a new meaning. Sharon taught me a lot in five days, especially how we don't know our future and we should always be there for one another in the present.

* * *

from Keith, Nurse...

I tried not to get too attached, not to get too close, but it's impossible. They stay with us, they touch us, pass through our lives and we through theirs. We cared for them and took care of them. It's hard when we lose them.

* * *

from Carol, Unit Clerk...

Buster was one of our residents for 25 years. He was one of the original residents to enter our facility as it opened. He died three years ago. On his last day, he called for a number of us and, one by one, we each went in and said our good-bye. Then we all cried and cried together.

* * *

from Stella, Nurse...

We had a resident who was a nurse during her career. Her name was Sandra. She often refused to take her medication. But, if she saw other residents refuse their medication, it was like she became a nurse again. Sandra would tell them, "These medications are for our own betterment; to make us feel well. You must take them." Sandra taught me an important lesson. One morning she said to me, as she was accepting her medications, "Let me take this for the last time." To me, at the time, I thought she was telling me she was going to be refusing her medication again after this time. Sandra expired within two hours. I think of her often and I hear my residents better because of her. In your life do not take anything for granted.

* * *

from Patricia, CNA...

Jerome was the first resident I ever lost. It tore me up. I took care of him for six months. We became close. He was part of my family. Jerome passed seven years ago, but I still remember the night he died. I was sitting by his bedside, holding his hand and I just closed my eyes for maybe five seconds. When I opened them, he was gone. I cried, I mean, really, just sat and wept.

* * *

from Waltina, COTA…

Jane was a beautiful spirit. She was soothing to us, always saying, "Come here, baby, you work so hard." We took care of her for six months. Her daughter had been in a coma and died while Jane was with us. Her son was coming the next day to escort Jane to her daughter's funeral. I went to see her and offered to polish her nails (she loved it when we would sit, talk and paint). She declined. Told me, "I won't need them done. I can't go to bury my baby. Just leave them. I'm telling you I won't need them done." I came in early the next morning to see her and offer support. She was gone; died peacefully in her sleep. That was two years ago. She's still with me.

* * *

from Alejandra, CNA…

Trixie was always smiling. She enjoyed singing and talking about God. I went to visit her in the hospital on my day off. This was just three weeks ago. It was our time together. I sat by her bedside and held her hand. Trixie lay in her bed, repeating softly, "Lord help me. I praise you, Lord. Help me Lord." She made good eye contact with me but never spoke a word other than those three sentences. We just sat together and then she passed. It was so sad. Trixie really touched me.

* * *

from Pamela, CNA...

Roger and I became very close. He was admitted to the nursing home on a number of occasions. Each time his daughter would request me as his aide. Then Roger came for the last time. He was very sick. For two years I took care of Roger the best as I know how. I will never forget his last day. In the morning he said, "God, let me die." We talked. Roger was ready. That afternoon he told his daughter, "Go, I'm going to be OK." His daughter said goodbye. I fixed him up in the bed as comfortable as could be and Roger passed a little while after. His daughter still calls me at home to this day.

* * *

from Diahnn, CNA...

We should talk about post-mortem care. For me it is as if they are still alive. I wash them, perfume them, gently, as though they can still feel my touch. It is the cycle of life. I don't want them to suffer. We do everything to keep them comfortable.

* * *

from Sharon, CNA...

"I feel like I know Gordon for so long. He's only been here for three weeks. He came here to die. He knows that. "I am not afraid, if you are here with me, I don't think I am going to die." Even though I just met him, I will take it very hard when Gordon passes away.

* * *

from Catherine, CNA...

Monique never called me by name. It was always, "That voice, I hear that voice," or "I know that voice." We used to go to church together on my Sundays off. One day Monique called me, "Catherine", three times. And she passed that night. Losing her took a lot out of me. It takes a toll when we lose them. I cry a lot.

* * *

from Dorothy, Nurse...

We took care of Debbie for one year. That was twelve years ago and I remember her like it was yesterday. Debbie was comatose. Still, I always spoke to her while I gave her care; about the weather, her family, my family, anything. She had three daughters and two sons, one of whom lived out of state. One day one of the daughters told me that her brother was flying in to visit. The whole family was planning to come to the nursing home together. For a week I would remind Debbie about the visit, naming each of her children and counting down the days.

On the morning of the visit, I was getting her ready and telling her one last time of the day's event. Out of nowhere, Debbie opened her eyes and asked, "When are they coming?" She startled me, to say the least. I got a staff member to stay with her and keep talking with her while I called her family to update them. They came immediately. It was a beautiful visit. Everyone speaking with their mom for the first time after a year's worth of daily visits. The next day Debbie died. She waited for everyone to be together and gave them such a gift. I felt so good for the family.

* * *

from Leslie, Social Worker...

It was something I needed to do, but it was difficult. I watched the aide wash and wrap the body ever so gently. What struck me was that she spoke to the resident the whole time. While it was certainly a solemn, respectful occasion, there was such a warmth to the way the CNA provided care. Being there helped me to be more available to the needs of dying residents. As difficult as it was, I am grateful for the experience.

* * *

from Carla, CNA...

I always looked forward to seeing Elisha. She was a most interesting person. A CNA by training, Elisha said, "The care you give me is the care I always gave to my residents." We would sit and talk—on my break time, before and after my shifts. Elisha had a way of making me feel my job is important.

She gave me a real gift. Elisha prepared me for her death. We talked about what a good life she had, how she had no regrets and was at peace. She was smiling the entire time I gave her care for the last time. Minutes later, Elisha was gone. I think of her often, yet never with sadness. Elisha gave me that.

* * *

from Imogene, CNA...

Maria was cute and troublesome. She was a good friend of mine. Even though she only spoke Spanish and I only speak English, I understood Maria and she understood me. She was a good friend of mine, a good friend. Her eyes, I remember her eyes at the end. They said, "Help me, I'm scared." I held Maria's hand and told her, "God be with you, where you are going is a better place." I stayed with her and she passed.

* * *

from Tom, Therapeutic Recreation Leader...

Ted has been deceased for thirteen years. I still have a picture of us on my office wall. He was only seven years older than me. His death taught me a lesson early in my career; one I am embarrassed now to have needed. Ted and I played chess regularly. I can remember playing chess like it was yesterday. He got sick and died within a week's time. Ted had been in a wheelchair for the five years I knew him. This is where my lesson comes in. Seeing him in his casket, like you, me, everybody else, reminded me to see the person, not the disability. Ted's death normalized him for me. I think of him all the time. Very humbling.

* * *

from Mary Lee, Nurse...

One resident I will never forget is Mildred. This was one strong woman. We took care of Mildred for four years and we lost her a year ago. I learned from her. Mildred used to pray when I would go to see her in her room. Even as she was actively dying, her prayer was always the same. First, she'd ask blessings for the other residents, second, blessings for the staff, and last, forgiveness for her wrongs. I think of Mildred often and try my best to follow her example.

* * *

from Nadine, Nurse...

I will always remember Greg. He was admitted one late afternoon and I arrived for work the next morning. Greg had not eaten, he'd refused, and had not allowed anyone to wash him. I went to his room. "I don't like the way you look, how 'bout I clean you up," I announced with a big smile, hiding my trepidation. "Okay," was all he said. That was all I needed. I washed him, dressed him, fed him and gave him his medication. Ten minutes later, Greg was dead. He taught me that we never know. We never know when we're giving care to someone for the last time. Do it well. I will always remember Greg.

* * *

from Phyllis, Unit Clerk...

Bertrand was like a family member, so close to me. Once, when I went on vacation, Bertrand refused to shower. When I came back he told me, "I was worried you ran away with another guy." I told him to bathe right now or I would leave him. We laughed and Bertrand showered. At the end, Bertrand was in the hospital. I visited every day. He said to the nurse in the hospital, "This is my wife, we'll get married here." I lost Bertrand six years ago. It is still very sad for me.

* * *

from Lucy, Medical Records Clerk...

You never know what life will bring. Melinda visited her brother Thomas twice a week. She was very dedicated to him and even interacted with other residents. She was "a regular" on the unit. Then two weeks passed with no Melinda. Next day, she was admitted to the nursing home—on the same floor as her brother. She was dying. This beautiful, vibrant woman was suddenly dying and, within weeks, deceased. I used to sit with her, holding her hands and talking. I got so attached to Melinda. I was devastated when she passed. I still get chills all over my body when I think of her.

* * *

from Maura, Dietician…

Vicki lived with us for four years. She was never a great eater. I fed her daily and we would talk. I was with Vicki when she took her last breath. We were holding hands and I said a prayer. Her CNA was singing a hymn to her when Vicki bid us goodbye. I will never forget her.

* * *

from Irma, CNA…

Pops died on his wife's birthday. He passed so peacefully, as his wife arrived. The sun was shining through the window onto his bed. Pops was lying, raised his hands over his head and breathed his last breath. We just held each other and cried. I miss both of them.

* * *

from Marva, CNA…

Candice was not a talker. We would sit quietly at times. Now Candice was dying. I arrived for my 11PM shift. My co-workers told me, "Candice is not well, we think she's waiting for you." Straight to her room and I gave her care. Then I sat, holding her hand. And Candice passed. On our time.

* * *

from Margaret, CNA...

I fed Sherice this one morning, just like any other morning, or so I thought. "You were the first to give me a shower here and you will be the last to give me a shower here," she said to me. Her words were chilling, real chilling. I didn't want to think about it. For three years I'd cared for Sherice, from the day she arrived. "Thank you for showing me the way to go back home," she continued. It took all of my energy not to cry. Sherice was not any sicker than she'd been before, but she never spoke like this. I told the nurse and we called her niece. Her niece came in, had a nice visit, but it was so sad. Sherice, she passed the next day. I couldn't believe it. She knew it was happening. I miss Sherice so much.

* * *

from Clover, CNA...

Twelve years ago I lost Sylvia. Saw her through good times and bad. "This time I will be going; I will wait for you to come back from your days off," she said. Two days later I returned. Sylvia told me she didn't want breakfast, but I was to go serve in the dining room, and then come see her. When I sat beside her our eyes met. Two seconds later her eyes closed. Sylvia was gone. She had waited for me. I cried so much. Part of my family, part of me, was gone.

* * *

from Camilla, Nurse...

I love the elderly. I get tearful when I think of them. We lose so many of them, you know. It's hard. I don't like good-byes, but they are important.

Our tutor in Nursing school in England always had this to say about post-mortem care: "Treat that person after they pass as if they were still living and breathing. Wash them and wrap them with dignity. Remember, they are still your resident and this is the last thing you will do for them." I've always taught my staff to give post- mortem care with reverence. They do and I'm very proud of them.

* * *

from Marvet, CNA...

I always admired Matthew. We got so close. He would give me money to shop for him and would watch me through his window to make sure I was safe. We developed such a bond. I would take my lunch breaks with him and sit and talk. Matthew would tell other staff members, "You're just jealous", and we would all laugh. We lost him eight years ago. I had to borrow a black dress from my sister to attend his funeral. I was so sad. I still have dreams about Matthew. I miss him.

* * *

from Elithia, Nurse...

I love Hilary. She was difficult, demanding, jealous of other residents and I love her. If she heard me say, "Hi", to her roommate, it was a big problem. You couldn't help but feel for her. Years later, as she lay dying, she whispered into my ear, barely audible, "I love you." We sat and held hands. It was so touching to me. I thought that would be our last night together, but Hilary was waiting for me when I arrived for my next shift. She passed that night. I was glad to be there with her and to provide her postmortem care. I remember her so well.

* * *

from Rachael, Nurse...

Cleo was 104 years old and attended church every day. He was a quiet gentleman and we developed a real closeness. Cleo passed away about an hour before my shift began. When the Nurse informed me, I started to cry. I remember thinking, "Why didn't he wait for me?" Silly, huh? I would have wanted to be with him. When his family arrived, we spent time together with Cleo in his room. I was able to assist his CNA with preparing his body. I still think of him often, even though he is gone one year.

* * *

from Paulette, CNA...

We were preparing Joycelyn for discharge home. She was leaving us the day before Thanksgiving and was so happy she'd done well enough to get home for the holidays. Joycelyn was always upbeat. When I arrived each night at 11 p.m., she would be waiting for me to fill me in on how her day had gone. She was very special. At 4:45 a.m. on Tuesday, she rang her call bell. It was the last thing she ever did. When I got to her room she was gone. We were expecting a nice goodbye the next day. Every now and then I think of Joycelyn and I wonder why.

* * *

from Daphne, CNA...

One day when I arrived at work, Doris told me about the death of another resident. It hurt me so much to hear the news. Doris put her arms around me and we cried and talked. After all the taking care of her I'd done, there was Doris, taking care of me.

* * *

from Larry, Dietary Aide...

The first resident I lost was Carla. She was a sweet lady. Losing her hurt me a lot. I hadn't realized how close I had come to our residents. I cried. Told myself not to get so close; but I can't help it. You get really attached and it hurts when we lose them.

* * *

from Margaret, CNA...

Lori was the first resident I ever took care of; a sweet, non-verbal 94-year-old lady. I grew to love her. We were very attached. I took a couple of days off and she died while I was away. For all the good times we had together, this is still what I remember: that I wasn't there when she passed. It's the worst feeling, knowing I wasn't there.

* * *

from Enid, CNA, Unit Clerk...

It still hurts like it was yesterday. I think of Sheena often. On this particular day I was assigned to the dining room for the shift. Sheena saw me walking trays to residents having breakfast in their rooms. She called my name and I went to her room to see her. I explained that someone else would give her care, as I was working the dining room. "Nobody else is touching me if you're here." I told her I would try, but I wasn't sure. And, as it turned out, I couldn't. There were other residents to feed and supervise. Reality that day was, someone else had the job of giving care to Sheena, or not, as she decided. Every now and then she would call my name. All the staff would stop in to offer help and explain my absence. A couple of hours later, she passed. It was, I mean, I felt it. If I had gotten the chance to wash and dress her, I'd feel better. It was like a final request. But I wasn't able to. It's been seven years and I can't forget her.

* * *

from Cynthia, CNA…

I'll tell you about Lisa. She reminded me of my mother— her features and her way of talking to you. She always called me, "my baby." I don't want to cry now. This is hard. What really hurt me was, she passed while I was on vacation. I wanted to be here with her, to tell her she'll be OK. That she's going to a better place. I didn't get to say my goodbye. That still hurts.

* * *

from Marie, CNA…

I was always "daughter," and Evelyn was always "Mom." It's been eight years since we lost her. Feels like yesterday talking about her. I was devastated. That morning, Evelyn had just gotten out of bed. As soon as she was in her chair she started asking to be placed back in bed. This was not normal for her. I am so happy to have made her comfortable, because a short time later she was gone. I always remember Evelyn.

* * *

from Garfield, Housekeeper...

Trudy died six years ago. I knew her for three years. "Hey, good looking," she would say as I came to clean her room. She was like a great-aunt, real nice. When Trudy died, it hurt like when you lose a family member. I told myself that was it, I wouldn't get close anymore; it hurts too much. I'm not doing well with that one. I can't help it; they pull you in.

* * *

from Heather, CNA...

Elizabeth and I got real close during the two years I cared for her. When she got sick, her behavior changed. Sometimes she was a completely different person, saying the most hurtful things to me. It hurt me to see my Elizabeth so sick and I always knew it wasn't her talking like that, it was her illness. Elizabeth passed on a day I was off and it still hurts that I wasn't there to say goodbye.

* * *

from Berryl, CNA...

Carrie was a very nice person. She would tell me, "You're so nice to me, you make me feel so good." I got so close to her. I was feeding her one afternoon and the nurse asked me to help her with something. I wasn't gone for three minutes. By the time I returned, Carrrie had passed away. Right there, sitting in her chair. It hurt me so much.

* * *

from Gwen, CNA…

When I first started, I tried not to get too attached. I didn't want to feel that kind of loss. Never did I think I would take my job so to heart. I look forward to coming here every day. Judy and Nadine are roommates. They both get jealous when I am giving care to the other. They don't like it; they yell at me, interrupt each other's conversation with me. I don't know what I'll do if I lose one of them.

* * *

from David, CNA…

Two years ago I lost a great lady. Justine and I would sit and chat about her past days. She even taught me how to comb her hair. "I am happy when you are on the job," she'd tell me. I wasn't at work when Justine died. Oh man, that bothered me. I wasn't home when my mother died, nor when my grandmother passed. And now, I wasn't here for Justine. That is a loss for me.

* * *

from Hyacinth, CNA…

Wilda was always kind. She talked to us like a grandmother. She even prayed for us. We took care of her for about a year. On the day of her funeral, I was off and had a number of scheduled appointments. I wore black all day and went to the funeral home as soon as I could. But I was late and the service was over. I am so disappointed I didn't get there to tell her family what a wonderful lady she was. I miss Wilda.

* * *

from Nana, Nurse...

I was Ken's CNA for two years and his Nurse for three years. We lost him two years ago. It really hurts me a lot, though being here the day he passed was good for me. I was able to take him to the morgue. I have a lot of grandmothers and grandfathers here and I hate to lose them.

* * *

from Agnes, CNA...

Carole was special. She had such a good sense of humor. As much as I knew I helped her, she helped me, too. Carole listened to you and gave good advice if you had a problem. It was a great loss when she passed. Just going back on the floor was hard.

* * *

from Elizabeth, Therapeutic Recreation Leader...

Tania was the first resident I lost. I will never forget her. I was home and called the hospital she was in to get her room number to go visit. The operator told me they had no such person. I called work, thinking she'd come home. The nurse told me she passed. I just cried for two hours. I was a wreck. I will never forget Tania.

* * *

from Herminia, Purchasing Agent…

John was an Adventist. One day, as I was singing and making rounds, he came out of his room and said, "I hope to see the face singing my hymns." That's how our six-year relationship began. I continued to stop by John's room and we'd sing together and talk about church. It took us back to our youth and reminded me of my father. John became such an important part of my life and I miss him. After time, there was nothing we couldn't tell each other.

As John became sick, I would sing to him. When he couldn't talk any more, he would just hold my arm. He was as much a comfort to me as I was to him. John and my dad were sick at the same time. One day, I sang my heart out. I must've sang 10 songs when I realized John had stopped patting my leg. He was gone. Later that day, I learned my Dad passed at the same time. That was sixteen years ago. I will never forget John. I still miss him.

* * *

from Janice, CNA…

I came onto the floor at 3 p.m. to start my shift. Made my rounds to say hello and see how all my residents were feeling. Lou said he wasn't feeling well. I told the nurse and we went to see Lou together. He was gone. He wasn't even sick. I learned then not to take life for granted. That was 18 years ago and he has remained with me all this time.

* * *

from Jackie, CNA…

Guy brought joy to me. He was a good man, though he had his moments. He could get very noisy on the unit and the other residents would tell him to be quiet. Guy would say, "This is the last stop for me and I'm gonna say all I have to say." To me he would ask, "I guess when I'm gone you're going to miss me?" And I do. He sticks with me. Guy's been gone five years. It was a joy to see him every day.

* * *

from Veronica, CNA…

Michelle and I were very close. I'm talking fifteen years ago. Still, I think of her often. Hers was a hard life. She and her family barely escaped Communist siege. Later, Michelle lost her son and husband within months of each other. She passed that same year, only two weeks after my dad died. I was here with her when she passed. I was a mess.

* * *

from Una, Nurse…

They are always with me. It was so sad. We took care of a 30- year- old woman named Maxine. She had a six-year-old son. He cried so hard when his mom died. He told me, "My mom's doctor told her not to have any kids; she would get sick. It's my fault my mom died." We stayed in contact with his grandparents for a while. I always wonder what became of that little boy.

* * *

from Myrna, Nurse…

Glenda was a nurse by profession. She was 60 years old when she came to us five months ago. Shortly after arriving, Glenda decided to forego any more treatment. Cognitively intact, she was aware of her prognosis. All we could do was keep Glenda as comfortable as possible. The entire team was touched by this strong, courageous woman. We asked her what her favorite place to be was, and she said, "The sea." And so her room was transformed into an underwater world. Everyone came in on their own time to paint. Glenda loved it. She passed very quietly soon after.

* * *

from Charles, Chaplain…

Monica was very fascinating to me. At 97 years old she was a daily reader of the *New York Times*. A fashion designer by trade, a published author, Monica was an intense person. I remember her keen interest in the inauguration of George Bush. Thinking we were to engage in a political conversation, I laughed so much when Monica explained that she was waiting with much anticipation to see what Laura Bush would be wearing.

This rather intense person became so quiet and calm as her end neared. One day we had a long chat. When I arrived and inquired if Monica knew who was there with her, she answered, "Surely, I know who you are." I asked if she was comfortable, peaceful. Monica replied, "Yes, I am very peaceful." Later, I asked if she was aware her life was slowly coming to its end. Monica said, "Yes, and I will remember you where I go."